YOUR *Blissful* LIFE

Timothy A. McGinty

Copyright © 2008 Timothy A. McGinty

ALSO BY TIMOTHY A. MCGINTY:

Wake-Up...Live the Life You Love
(Co-Author)

Wake Up Publishing
Murray, KY 42071

COPYRIGHT © 2009 by Timothy A. McGinty

Pre-press Management by New Caledonian Press
Text Design: K-Squared Designs, LLC. www.k2ds.com

Printed in the United States of America.
All rights reserved. Except as permitted under the U.S. Copyright Act of 1976, no part of this publication may be reproduced, distributed, or transmitted in any form or by any means, or stored in a database or retrieval system, without the prior written permission of the publisher.

Publisher Operations: Wake Up Publishing
P.O. Box 894
Murray, KY 42071
270.753.5225 USA

Library of Congress Cataloguing in Publication Data
Your Blissful Life
ISBN-978-1-933063-21-8

To my mother, who inspired and believed in me, until her passing. She was an awesome woman who raised six beautiful children, giving each exactly what they needed most: her unconditional love!

Thank you, Mom!

CORRINE E. MCGINTY
JUNE 9, 1932 - JUNE 4, 2007

To my father, who pushes me to be my best even when I don't want to. He was, and continues to be, an inspiration to me. His strength and support are priceless.

Thanks, Dad!

Table of Contents

Foreword
Preface
Acknowledgements
Introduction

Why Are You Here?
Chapter 1 Your Struggle Within
Chapter 2 Recognition and Acceptance
Chapter 3 Your Decision to Act

Your Pathway
Chapter 4 Your Definition
Chapter 5 Your Discovery
Chapter 6 Your Acceptance

Your Walk
Chapter 7 Your Commitment
Chapter 8 Your Action
Chapter 9 Your Achievement

Your Maintenance
Chapter 10 Your Changes
Chapter 11 Your Integration
Chapter 12 Your New Place

Epilogue

Foreword

I am honored to have been asked to contribute to Timothy McGinty's amazing book. It is nothing less than exciting to be even a small part of this dynamic road map to a better life.

Tim McGinty is intrigued by the ways in which people cope, adapt and, finally excel in life. Based on his own discovery of self, Tim decided he had actually discovered something much more important. He then put the principles and strategies he had found into action and discovered that he was the owner of a Blissful Life.

His Blissful Life, however, was not a magical gift. It was not a discovery such as a beautiful view or a giant diamond waiting to be found by the side of a path. This life was not achieved by accident or without sacrifice. He turned away from mainstream thought and action to develop a life lived on purpose. That kind of discovery can be unsettling, at times, or even threatening to yourself or others around you.

Now he has brought that same discovery to others through his writing. The book moves the reader through a process to achieve a Blissful Life. Tim does this by providing an essay of information and introspection followed by a series of questions that aid the reader in narrowing the focus and creating a plan of action.

Tim's writing is filled with encouragement. He addresses his reader conversationally, which allows the reader to be at ease with the prospect of change and to take heart from someone who has "been there."

He believes absolutely that this kind of life is available to everyone. His sincerest desire is to help, as his impressive list of coaching clients demonstrates. Now, he has placed his strategy and his faith between the covers of this book. The rest is up to you.

-Steven E
Creator of the *Wake Up...Live the Life You Love* series

When Tim McGinty asked me if I would write a foreword to his new book, *"Your Blissful Life,"* I was thrilled. Tim and I have known each other for some years now. I have had the privilege to observe Tim re-engineer his life, grow two successful practices and, all the while, create a *Blissful Life* for himself. It has been said that when the student is ready, the teacher appears. Tim and I had a conversation in 2006 in which Tim mentioned to me that he was considering changing the focus of his business. He asked for my recommendations. While I offered him a few suggestions, it was Tim who ultimately made it happen. You could say that I was the teacher who appeared because Tim was ready.

The most difficult thing to achieve in life is balance. Juggling your personal and professional pursuits while maintaining your sense of self is the ultimate achievement and one that Tim has accomplished brilliantly. That you are reading this book must mean you, too, are ready for a *Blissful Life*. That you are reading this book also means that your teacher has now appeared. That teacher is Timothy A. McGinty.

Tim has captured the essence of defining, planning and integrating a method for attaining a *Blissful Life*. This book will guide you through the simple steps for achieving happiness and fulfillment. Note that I said the steps are simple. Note that I did not say that it is easy. When things are uncomfortable, you need a coach to hold you accountable and get you through the rough spots. This book is your portable coach.

Don't just read this book, devour it! This book had a profound effect on me and I am sure it will have a similar effect on you. Enjoy the process of creating your *Blissful Life* and I look forward to hearing the wonderful stories that will no doubt be created as a result of this book.

Warm regards,

-Carl L. Gould
Author of *Blueprint for Success* and *The 7 Stages of Small Business Success*.
Founder and creator of CMT International,
the farthest-reaching business mentoring organization in the world.
Riverdale, NJ, USA

I personally saw Tim's level of expertise and ability to bring clarity and understanding to what drives human performance in his work with the Anthony Robbins Companies. So many of the people I work with are busy struggling to achieve a successful life, but their definition of success is often someone else's definition; one of accumulation of wealth, power, achievement or a hundred other things motivated by a world that markets such things to all of us as the ultimate measures of "success." *Your Blissful Life* holds the potential to show any reader how the pursuit of hollow, temporal or impermanent things such as these can lead us away from the true happiness that awaits us all...happiness that is captured in Tim's approach to achieving a life not just of survival, but one of true bliss.

-Jay Niblick
Author *Blueprint for Success* and *What's Your Genius?*
CEO Innermetrix Incorporated

Many of us go through life unsuccessfully searching for that elusive feeling of happiness and bliss. Tim McGinty has revealed a step-by-step formula for evaluating each part of your life and developing a plan to achieve what few people ever find. If you feel that part of your life is out of balance, or if you have not reached your full potential, Tim gives you the steps to find true happiness. With this book he reveals his personal quest for happiness and how he used this method to find it. It works! However, you can't just wish for happiness...you have to put forth an effort. The first step is to read the book and complete the action steps at the end of each chapter. If you really desire true bliss, you'll find the action steps to be thought-provoking and helpful. Enjoy the journey. I did. Thanks, Tim. Many people are going to live more fulfilling and happier lives because of your book.

-Dr. Dennis J. Hocker, P.E.
Chairman & CEO
Genesis Capital Group, Inc.

The image of an onion has changed my life.

What kind of bizarre statement is that? And how does it possibly relate to a book on self-discovery?

I would have echoed that same sentiment over a year ago. But over a year ago, I had not yet made the decision to work with Tim McGinty as my business advisor and coach.

As you will see for yourself when reading this book, Tim likens the process of self-discovery to peeling back the layers of an onion...going deeper and deeper toward the very core, the very essence of the onion, the very essence of *you*.

I've known Tim for several years. Our businesses and involvement in local chambers of commerce has brought us in and out of contact as those years have gone by.

In January 2007, Tim called to invite me to sit on the Board of Directors for a chapter of the Entrepreneurs Club of America he had founded. Oddly enough, I had been planning to call him as well because after 13 years in business I had decided that I needed help in taking my graphic design business to the next level. So, as we enjoyed lunch at a local establishment a week later, I found myself enthusiastically hiring him as my advisor.

A few days later, a document from Tim arrived in my e-mail inbox with instructions to carefully think through and then answer the questions contained therein. (You will find these questions and their process in Chapter 5 of this book.) I had no idea what this had to do with growing my business. I was a bit taken aback. Answering questions about what I "really" wanted out of life was not at all what I expected and, honestly, it irritated me. "Let's just get on with this already!" I thought. "Obviously I already know what I want, that's why I called him in the first place!"

Nonetheless, I sat down and worked my way through the questions.

Looking back on it now, aside from my irritation, I didn't feel much of anything that first time through.

"First time through?" you say. Yes, the first time through.

Tim is not kidding when he talks about peeling the onion. Just like an onion, my outer layers were dry and tough. What an image! Nonetheless, it was true, and just like an onion, the really good part lies just under the surface of those tough, dry layers.

With his guidance, I kept peeling, and started to really feel the thrill of dreams again...the excitement of what I could make happen for myself.

As he helped me work through the self-discovery process, to my amazement, I found that I wanted something very different from what I had answered the first time. Luckily, Tim was talented and insightful enough to know this and to keep me "peeling," so to speak.

Eventually, I did get to the truth of what I really wanted from my life, and it set me off on a path I would never have dreamed of six months prior to this experience. It is one that I am enjoying thoroughly today...one that I am more excited about than I have been over anything else in a long time. It is a very good feeling. This is what you have to look forward to when delving into this book.

I am so happy that Tim has decided to put his process into writing and to share it with others.

He has a remarkable talent for what he does, and he has true empathy for his clients, which comes through in his coaching style. His energy is downright infectious and his positive outlook on life stirs dreams deep down in your very core.

You are about to embark on a great journey. Enjoy every moment!

-Kelly V. Pavlovic
President, Feather & Stone Designs
March 2008

Preface

This book was written to provide you with the method for discovering what you truly want your life to be like. Too often, the average person cannot afford one-on-one life coaching services, or to attend workshops and retreats. Instead, they struggle on a daily basis, being frustrated, angry, and often times depressed, until they stop seeking.

Many of my clients have told me they sought out a coach because they felt as if life had passed them by. They expressed this either after a workshop I taught or during the one-hour complimentary coaching session I offer coaching prospects. The most interesting thing is that it did not matter who they were, they all felt the same way! They were mothers, fathers, brothers, sisters, investment brokers, social workers, real estate agents, teachers, firemen, lawyers; the list goes on and on. Before working with me, they felt there was no such thing as true happiness or that they simply could not have it. They soon realized life hadn't passed them by! Anyone can have the truly happy life they are seeking!

Help has arrived! This book will enable you to understand why you are where you are in life, and why you feel the way you do at this very moment. It will also enable you to accept it. I then take you by the hand and walk you through a method to define your blissful life for every part of your being. During your journey, I provide guidance through the sharing of my experiences using this method in discovering my blissful life. You then define exactly what it is you want in each part of your life and the balance you want between these parts. I then walk you through the method for defining your action plan to achieve happiness and balance in your external life. I have used this process with my coaching clients over the years. Each quickly discovered they still had dreams and these dreams were, in fact, attainable! Using this process, they defined their unique path to happiness and then walked their path. I call the happiness and balance each seeks a blissful life. Finally, I will present a method for maintaining your blissful life.

Enjoy your journey!

-Timothy A. McGinty

Acknowledgments

I'd like to acknowledge the founders of NLP, Richard Bandler and John Grinder. Without them, my discovery and this book, would not be possible. Also, Michael Bennett and Kaileen Sherk of Bennett-Stellar University. Without them I would still be searching for my own "Blissful Life."

I would also like to thank all of the coaches and mentors who assisted me on my journey in discovering my blissful life. You are an awesome group, each with your own unique talents and contributions into this work. I learned much from each and every one of you.

Finally, I wish to acknowledge all of my past and current clients. I have learned something from each and every one of you. Thank you for allowing me to assist you in your journey.

Introduction

Have you ever noticed that some that some people always seem to be happy, while others always seem to be struggling or unhappy? If you don't know anyone like this, it is okay! This just means that you have surrounded yourself with others who are just like you. This is very common because it gives us comfort...comfort in knowing we are not alone. What do these people know that others do not? Why is it that they do not seem to be impacted by life's many challenges? If they are impacted, how is it that they are able to overcome any and everything that life throws their way? How is all of this possible when others are constantly run over by the truck called "life?" Why can't those who are struggling or unhappy do what others do? Why are they unhappy? Why do they feel like they are merely surviving, instead of living life to its fullest?

The reason you feel this way is simple: you haven't been taught to discover what you want for every part of your life and how to develop an action plan for achieving it. Just as a house has many rooms, your life is made up of various parts. If you don't like how a room looks, you first define what you want it to be and then take action to make it the way you want. Your life is the same! First, you need to define the parts and then rank them in order of importance to you. Those that are most important are your essential parts. Those that are less important are your accessory parts. Just as with rooms in your home, define exactly what you want the parts to be and what you need to do to make this a reality. This book gives you precisely that.

After reading this book, you will know exactly what you want in your life, in what balance, what you need to do to get it and how to maintain it! Knowing what you want is big, but knowing what you need to do and doing it is huge! This is the secret to getting everything you want, just the way you want it.

You're going to love this journey. You have finally found the tool that enables you to define what you want in your life, the balance you seek, what you will need to do to get it, and how to maintain it. You are finally going to be focusing on you! The greatest joy is discovering and living your life the way you want, on your own terms! To do so, you must be open and honest with yourself. This enables you to discover your deepest desires, wants, and needs. Remember, all things are possible! My clients, no matter their state at the beginning of their journey, found a blissful life by using this process. Using this process can be that powerful force that others see and say, "Wow! I want to be like that!"

1

Your Struggle Within

Why Are You Here?

For years, it seemed as though happiness...true happiness or as I call it, blissfulness, was missing in my life. You see, the more focused and the harder I tried to define and catch this bliss, the further it seemed to move away. Does this sound familiar to you? Perhaps I just described you or someone you know, a brother, sister, mother, father, significant other or friend of yours. One may be in a very lonely and frustrating place. Typically, these people are struggling to define exactly what it is they want in their life that will provide them bliss.

So what is the difference between being happy and being blissful? Happiness is when you go through life not quite living it to its fullest. For some reason, you feel certain parts of your life should be better, but you aren't sure why they fail to be. There seems to be something missing, but you're not sure what that something is. Blissful means you love life, every second of every day, living in the moment, loving it no matter what. You live for each moment embracing all the beauty that it brings. I wrote this book to share with you the process I used to discover bliss and maintain it in my life. Deep within all of us lies the desire for blissfulness.

The main reason people are struggling to find bliss is because there hasn't been a tool to assist them in their discovery. That may have been true, until now! This book sends you on the path to discovering your own true happiness, or as I refer to it..."Your Blissful Life."

At the conclusion of each chapter, you will find a series of questions that will allow you to focus during your journey toward your blissful life. Enjoy your discovery!

The Struggle Within

Ah, the struggle. Certainly, at one time or another, we have all experienced it. Regardless of age, race, sex, religion or socio-economic status, we have all struggled. We are torn. It may appear at times that others have never struggled with anything or are moving on with their lives. Sooner or later what they realize is that they are spinning in place, going nowhere. They will not move forward until they too recognize, accept, and deal with the struggle which is unique to each individual. Sooner or later, it affects everyone in one form or another. Dealing with the struggle takes more than just thought and action. If it were simple, you wouldn't need this book. But it isn't! The struggle is a very complex thing, just as you are a very complex person. You have many different facets and the struggle can rear its head in any single part that uniquely defines you. This struggle is likely rocking you at the core of who you are.

So, what exactly is a part of your life? A "part" is the name given to the various components of your life. These components can be either internal or external. Some examples of external parts are your significant other, your career, friends and family. Some examples of your internal parts are your spiritual self, your self-confidence, ego, self-direction (your master plan for your life), your religious self and even your internal way of thinking. You know that little voice in the back of your head that is always tossing in thoughts of gloom and doom. It is that voice inside your head that is telling you right now you cannot have a blissful life. This inner voice is part of your sub-conscious mind. It is a result of years of learning and experiencing less than useful patterns. What is your subconscious mind? It is the part of your brain which allows you to breathe without having to think. Your diaphragm moves up and down, forcing air into and out of your lungs. Breathing is an "auto-pilot" type of function...one that your mind does not need to focus on to control. Your mind is also on auto-pilot when doing common tasks such as placing a key into a lock. Rarely, if ever, do you have to tell yourself how to put the key in the lock, you just do it. These functions are all controlled by your subconscious mind.

It permits you to do things without having to think about it.

You are made up of a large number of parts. By this I mean that today you may define yourself by a certain number of parts and then realize more as you continue to grow and learn. Parts may also be either in your conscious or subconscious mind. So, to what part of us can the struggle attach itself? It can attach itself to any part, and for some, to all parts! If attached to every part, the struggle can become overwhelming. Some people view their lives as being a series of never ending struggles! They will forever remain exactly where they are until they recognize and deal with the struggle that has engulfed their lives. They will expend all of their energies simply to remain where they are, struggling to keep their heads above water! The most amazing thing about parts is that they are all unique and, most importantly, they are *you*! You are the one who defines your parts and what they mean in your life.

The emotions we feel are a direct result of how we perceive our parts. Emotions are our deepest feelings. Often, people first begin to realize their struggle when the emotions tied to each part starts to conflict with other parts. The struggle is unique for everyone. We all experience different levels of conflict, emotions and behavior. The struggle becomes most intense when you experience it in multiple parts of yourself at once. The more parts are affected, the more intense the struggle. Wow! It is no wonder, then, that this can be so overwhelming. The reason you are reading this book is for assistance in overcoming it.

How do you know if you are having the struggle? You can recognize this by certain indicators: emotions and thoughts. Our thoughts and emotions are indicators of how we feel about our parts. In every instance, you are the sole person involved. The struggle is an internal battle, though external forces may influence it. If you are not at complete and total peace with yourself, you are, in some way, dealing with the struggle.

Here is an example. When I was young, I did not know anything about the struggle. However, I felt that I was different in many ways than my friends and family. I was not sure how or why, but I knew I was different. I did not concern myself with whether or not this difference was right, wrong, good or bad; I just knew what I felt and knew it made me unique.

Years later, during the height of my professional career, I was very successful as a co-owner of an information technology company. We had started the organization from the ground up and had received many awards. These awards ranged from community involvement to customer satisfaction and were recognized as one of the fastest growing organizations in northeast Ohio. As I stood in my office one day it hit me. Feelings from my youth came racing back to the forefront of my mind...from subconscious to conscious. Despite the success I was experiencing and the many awards we had won, something was amiss. I should have been ecstatic, but something was not quite right. Though I was not sure what it was or how to discover it, I was certainly struggling with it. My struggle led me through much research, learning and discovering my blissful life. Additionally, it led to writing this book to assist you in recognizing, accepting and deciding to move on in your struggle.

What is your struggle? You must be honest with yourself. The journey you are about to embark upon is purely for yourself. It is okay to focus on yourself. Most of us spend our time focused on others. This is how we were raised and what we learned from society, but here is the opportunity to focus on yourself to discover and define your blissful life. Once discovered, your blissful life will impact every part of you, enabling you to live the life you desire!

List all of your parts that are important to you.

Which part or parts create a struggle for you?

Are any parts connected to one another?

2 Recognition and Acceptance

You must accept your struggle with all your heart and soul. Embrace your struggle. It is a part of you and makes you unique. Millions of people just like you are currently in the process of experiencing difficulties. You are not alone! Everyone at one time or another will deal with the struggle. Many people deny or ignore their struggle. They go through life frustrated, angry, depressed, uncertain and lonely.

Your thoughts, feelings and views are neither good nor bad, right nor wrong. They simply are what they are: your thoughts, feelings and views. At this point, accepting this fact is a key part in moving forward and discovering your blissful life. Put aside any judgment you or others have made.

Refuse to judge yourself! When we judge ourselves, we place ourselves in a box. Typically, these boxes are very restrictive. Many judgments are based on our own or someone else's standards...standards that may not be useful. However, when we refuse to judge ourselves, we accept ourselves for who we are...unconditionally. When we truly accept ourselves, we then begin to truly love and embrace ourselves. Only then can we begin to improve. This acceptance enables you to have unlimited potential to become whatever you want.

I want you to know that it is okay to be dealing with the struggle. Accept yourself for who you are at this point in your life. All of your experiences at this juncture have made you who are. Some of these experiences were more enjoyable than others. But you have learned a great deal as a result. Accept yourself! Enjoy your unique position on earth.

While I recognized my uniqueness at an early age, I learned to suppress it to fit in. I mastered how to operate in their world. However, without realizing it, my subconscious mind was not letting go. No matter how far I repressed it or how successful I was operating in this world, my struggle was still with me. Their definition of success was not *my* definition. Mine was much larger. It was not until my a-ha moment while standing in my office did I realize how truly important my uniqueness was! It was then I decided to embrace my uniqueness and gave myself permission to encourage and nurture it. All these years...forty plus...had led me to this place, this moment of total acceptance. I had just experienced the most empowering event of my life because I finally recognized and accepted my uniqueness. You are also working your way through the same process.

The following questions will assist you in recognizing exactly where you are in your life. They will also assist you in recognizing your struggle. The more honest and open you are with yourself the faster you will recognize and accept your struggle. Remember, this is a process that requires self reflection and honesty. In Chapter 1 you identified your most important parts and the connections between them. Enjoy your discovery as you answer the following questions.

Review your answers to the questions at the end of Chapter 1. If you did not note a struggle in your answers in Chapter 1, revisit each part of yourself and note any struggle you uncover.

Write a note to yourself explaining what you need to do to accept your struggle.

How do you feel about your struggle?

Do you accept your struggle unconditionally?

What will acceptance of your struggle give you?

What are you now able to hear, see or feel that you could not, prior to accepting your struggle?

What will the total acceptance of your struggle enable you to do in working your way through the process of discovering your blissful life?

3

Your Decision to Act

Now that you have learned what your struggle is and have accepted that you are dealing with it, it is time to take action to resolve your struggle. Most of us want to be at peace in our lives so much we will stop at nothing to achieve it. Dealing with and resolving your struggle now needs to be the main focus of your life. Resolving it is the most meaningful action one can take and once resolved, enables you to move towards your blissful life.

In reality, you have already made the decision to take action. By purchasing this book, you decided to take action on resolving your struggle to improve your life. Everyone makes these decisions on a daily basis, whether they choose to recognize it or not. With every action, decision or feeling, we decide how we move. Those that refuse to recognize or accept their struggle will move away from having to deal with it because it is a very emotional thing. While these decisions may feel good at the time, they ultimately prevent us from achieving our blissful life. Individuals like you and I who deal with our struggle will make more informed decisions to deal with the uncomfortable as we move towards the life we really desire.

Congratulations on taking the first steps toward resolving your struggle! Regardless of the reason or way in which you made your decision, the important point is that you are moving towards what you really want!

For me, the decision to take action was actually quite radical to those around me. You see, virtually everyone I knew viewed me as very successful and happy. I learned early on how to repress my uniqueness that was burning inside of me. When I decided to take action, I wasn't exactly what or why it was, but suddenly I knew I had to find the answers to both questions. Once I recognized that I was dealing with a struggle and fully accepted it, I had to take immediate action. It was as if I was being pulled by an incredible force within to move towards the life I always wanted and this was the first step. I had never experienced anything like it. I have to admit…at times I was scared. However, every time I felt fear, it was overcome by my desire to finally achieve the life I wanted to live. This fear was different than other fears. It had more to deal with me finally getting what I wanted, versus not. Deep down inside, I knew by doing this I would get exactly what I wanted. Nothing would get in my way. I had to have the answers!

So how was it that I was able to move past my fear? I was able to move past my fear once I learned that all fear is based on uncertainty. That's right, uncertainty! Uncertainty comes in many forms. It can be the outcome of a situation, how we feel about ourselves or where we are headed. Once I accepted that my fear was based purely on uncertainty, I was able to walk right past it because I knew I was going to discover whatever it is I needed to discover in order to resolve my struggle. It was now gone! What is it that you are uncertain about? What do you need to accept or realize to overcome this deficiency? How does your taking action towards discovering your blissful life give you certainty? Use these questions to disarm your uncertainty and gain the certainty you need to take actions you need to take!

As a result of moving past my fear, I had my partners buy out the company. Everyone thought I was crazy for doing it, but I didn't mind. Little did they know the real reason behind my decision: I was about to embark upon my life-changing discovery process. Many did not support me in my decision, but that was okay with me. I was doing this for me, not them. Others were totally jealous of my decision. They only wished that they had the wherewithal to take such actions. There was actually only a very small group that encouraged me to go out and grow as an individual. Regardless of the relation each person had to me, they made their assessment based on how much of themselves they saw in me. For me, leaving the environment in which I was operating was an important part of freeing myself. My experience in dealing with my struggles was the most enjoyable, fulfilling and meaningful journey of my life. Embrace your decision to move. You are headed in the direction of attaining what you desire more than anything else in the world. You are about to give yourself the greatest gift ever: a blissful life.

The remainder of this book will provide you with the process to follow for discovering, defining and detailing the actions you need to take to resolve your struggles and achieve your blissful life. Remember to be totally honest with yourself...totally accepting of the thoughts, feelings and views along your journey. It is *your unique journey*. Enjoy your personal discovery!

4

Your Definition

The next few steps of the process I refer to as Your Pathway. It is uniquely yours because you are doing all the work for one person...yourself. This will be work like you have never experienced it before. You will enjoy your work because you will be working on and for yourself. Your Pathway is made up of the following chapters:

Chapter 4:   Your Definition
Chapter 5:   Your Discovery
Chapter 6:   Your Acceptance

After completing this process, you will have defined a specific destination and begin moving toward it. This process is a repetitive one because while you use it initially to define your pathway, you will use it again and again in the future to maintain a blissful life. Enjoy building your pathway.

The beauty of the idea of my book, *Your Blissful Life,* is simple...it is all yours! Only *you* can define exactly what it means to you and the various parts of your life. There have never been two individuals who desired exactly the same thing. While they may share some common desires, they will have unique requirements for their respective blissful lives. Just as each of us is one-of-a-kind, so are our definitions of a blissful life. As you execute the process of defining your blissful life, you are creating your own unique path. It is much like a work of art, a newly built home or a room that you redo within your home. You are starting with a blank piece of paper or an empty plot of land. You then begin to define all the different parts that your work will require. You describe these things in detail before you pick up a paint brush, clear a tree of the land or buy any paint or wallpaper for your room. As you continue you pick up your paint brush and begin painting, you clear trees and set the foundation for your new home, or begin painting the room. You continue working until you have exactly what you want. Whether you realize it or not, you have created a unique piece of art that is all you. You're an artist! So, how can each of us have such a unique definition for the same objects of our desire?

As discussed earlier, we are all made up of many parts. Recall as well that all of these parts are unique to each and every one of us. It is because of this that we all place different values on our various parts. So what is value as it relates to each of us? Value is the importance we place on the various parts of our lives. How we value our various parts defines who we are and how we act. Our definitions and actions help us to define our self-esteem or self worth. How we value our parts also impacts our desires to have certain people or things in our lives. The truth is, how we value them drives our everyday actions. While I place a certain value or importance on my professional career, you may place a completely different value on yours. You may place greater importance on your relationship with your friends than you do on your profession. Everyone places a different value on a certain part than someone else will. This will impact how each of us treats our professions and friends. You and I will act differently in this example because of the value we place on these groups. Everyone will. How you value each of your parts is a large component of who you will become in the future.

The importance you place on your various parts defines who you are and how you act. More importantly, it also defines your blissful life. You are currently reading this book because you need to paint a new picture, build a new home or redo your room. This need is demonstrated through our dissatisfaction, frustration, or struggle with some part of ourselves or between parts of ourselves. You may feel a need to redefine or resolve a conflict within or between your parts or feel you need to define new parts and integrate them into yourself. Use this process repeatedly throughout your life because your values continue to change over time as you grow wiser and older. Most people value things differently than when they were young. As your value of your parts changes over time, so do you! This is how you identify, compare and take action on a daily basis. Every day you make decisions and take various actions based purely on how you value your parts! Everything you do is driven by the need to satisfy and achieve the value and definition you have for your parts which, when combined, define you as a person.

My blissful life meant creating a balance between my parts that allowed me to assist others in achieving their goals, while providing a satisfactory standard of living. It also meant that I have the freedom and permission from myself to continue to grow and discover more about myself and the world I live in. I feel that there are no silly ideas or paths. I have given myself permission to explore all of them, no matter where they might lead. I have learned that in order for me to live my blissful life, I must be true to myself, my ideals, my thoughts, my intuitions and my feelings. When I do this, I can do anything, be anything and discover anything I desire. When I am doing this while helping others to enrich their own lives, I am truly living my blissful life.

In order to achieve your blissful life, you need to allow yourself to explore all of your thoughts no matter how small or far-fetched you might think they are. Permit yourself to explore them and discover how much you value them. The more you allow yourself to explore and discover, the closer you will be to learning about your blissful life. There are many examples of people who have permitted themselves to discover and become anything they wanted. Musicians, ice skaters, gymnasts, athletes, executives, doctors, business owners, mothers, fathers and actors are all examples of people who have permitted themselves to discover themselves and their blissful life. Notice that each of the examples are uniquely different from one another and from my description of my blissful life. Yours will also be different too because it will be uniquely you! You too can achieve your blissful life by discovering and learning about yourself in a way you never have.

Review your list of parts from Chapter 1. Have you discovered any other parts? If so, note them here.

What part or parts from your list are most important (valuable) to you?

Why are your most important parts the most important to you?

5

Your Discovery

Now that you are aware that you are made up of various parts, have identified them and what they mean to you, it is time to focus on them. Remember to allow yourself to go wherever you need to go, explore whatever you need to explore, to learn whatever you need to learn. Give yourself the permission and freedom you need to focus on your parts. It is important to note that some individuals have found that their spiritual and religious selves are one and the same, while others feel they are separate. Both views are perfectly acceptable, as they are unique to each individual.

It is now time for you to take some time to discover your own, personal parts. There are many layers of parts, and just when you think you have identified all of them, you will discover more.

The discovery process is like peeling an onion. It is quite easy at first. The deeper and more detailed you get, the juicier it becomes. Like peeling of an onion, you will experience many different emotions. You will laugh, cry, wonder aloud and ultimately amaze yourself. This is okay; keep moving. You will get closer and closer to defining your blissful life with every step you take and with every emotion you allow yourself to experience. This is why I call this step of the journey "Your Discovery." Embrace your discoveries: they are uniquely your own!

When I went through my process of discovery, I initially identified the obvious parts of myself like brother, husband, friend, professional, bowler, golfer, etc. I easily accepted these parts. My journey became much more personal when I allowed myself to identify those parts I had hidden away like my intuitive self, religious self, spiritual self, creative self, and emotional self, to name a few. I really had to concentrate and allow myself to discover these parts as they were the parts that were the inner layers of my onion. I finally allowed myself to discover them during a Neuro-Linguistic Programming (NLP) Certification course I was taking in Sedona, Arizona. It was during this class that we had to go through an exercise in identifying all of our parts.

I had taken various self-help and coaching courses from industry leaders around the world in my quest to discover who I was and what I really wanted. Though I didn't realize it at the time, this was part of my journey to discover all of my parts. It was during the class in Sedona that I finally allowed myself to accept and discover all I needed in these deeper parts. Little did I know at the time that this course would change me forever! I had many emotions tied to these parts. I cried and laughed many times during my discovery of my inner layers. It was okay though because I gave myself permission to explore and discover them. I accepted them for what they were and what they mean to me. By giving myself permission and being totally accepting of these parts and emotions I was able to go where I needed to go to discover who I really was and wanted to become.

Many of my clients have been overcome by various emotions they experienced, such as happiness, fear, joy and sadness. They experience these emotions to such an extent they often need to stop to rest in order to focus more deeply on a particular part. This is okay too! Once they make these deeper discoveries they continue on their discovery. I compare this time to walking away from the onion because it has become so overpowering that you must rest your eyes until you can see clearly enough to continue peeling. During this time, your mind, body and spirit are also rejuvenated. I took time-outs during my discovery because it was a very emotional one for me. I used this time to understand what the part and the emotions I felt meant. This was a very reflective, personal time for me. I was surprised that I had learned to bury many of my deepest emotions of how I really felt about the various parts of myself. However, I promised I would permit myself to explore and discover whatever I needed in order to discover and resolve my struggle. I often wrestled with my discoveries.

Sometimes I was shocked because this was the first time I permitted myself to totally accept myself and my parts for what they were, parts of myself and my feelings about them. However, it was during these rest periods that I experienced my greatest growth! You too will continue to learn and grow during these periods. So take your time, discover, grow and continue at your own pace. You are getting closer to what you want.

As you move through "Your Discovery," you may identify even more parts, and this is normal, as it signifies growth. If you discover more parts during or after completing this section, simply come back to this chapter and define the new parts and their meaning. Then walk through the process again until you have defined all of your newly discovered parts. It is now time to define what your parts mean to you. This process is quite simple. What could possibly be easier or more fun than defining *you* to yourself? No one knows *you* better than you. For each part you identified in the previous chapters, answer each of the following questions. They will help you to define what you want; to know exactly when you have reached your blissful life.

Is there any part that you have pushed aside, even though it is truly important to you?

What does each part that you have identified mean to you?

Are there specific parts of your life in which you desire greater satisfaction? If so, what are they?

How does each of the parts you identified fit into your life?

FOR EACH PART, CONSIDER YOUR PREVIOUS ANSWERS.
TO ANSWER THE FOLLOWING FOR EACH OF YOUR PARTS.

What do you want in this specific part of your life?

Be very specific with the details in answering this question. For example: How much money do you want? Where you do want to live? What does your home look like? What do you hear? What feelings do you want to experience? How soon do you want these things in your life?

Where, when and with whom do you want this in this part of your life?

In what location will you be when you achieve this for your part? What is your timeline for achieving what you want? Are there any others involved in your goal? (Note: You should be in charge of achieving your goal, however others may be involved.)

How will you know when you have satisfied this specific part?

How will you measure your success? When and by what method will you determine that you have achieved your goal? Will you be living somewhere different, have more money in the bank, feel loved and accepted by someone or yourself?

How will others know that you have satisfied this specific part?

What will those around you be able to see, hear or feel once you have achieved your goal for this specific part? Will they see a new car, hear you laughing or feel better after being around you? These can be friends, lovers, relatives, acquaintances or co-workers. Everyone you come in contact with will notice the difference.

What changes will take place in your life if you get what you want for each part?

Compared to the present moment, what will be different in your life? What impact will getting what you want have on your life? How will your life be different than it is today?

_____
_____
_____
_____
_____
_____
_____
_____
_____
_____
_____
_____
_____
_____
_____
_____
_____
_____
_____
_____

What changes will occur if you don't get what you want for this part?

If you achieve only a part of the overall goal, what impact will this have on your life? What impact does getting only portions of what you want have on your life?

Is your goal for this part going to be worth the effort it will take to get it?

The time and effort spent on reaching your goal is linked with the effort necessary to achieve the goal. Are you willing to do what it takes...whatever it takes, no matter what...to reach your goal?

What does getting what you want for this part mean to your other parts?

This is your ecological test. How does getting what you want in this part, impact your other parts? Is it congruent with the rest of your desires? Can your other parts accept this part if you get what you want? If not, do you need to adjust anything? If so, how do you feel about it? Can you accept and live with the adjustment?

Now that you have named and clearly defined all of your parts, you need to rank them in order of importance. Knowing your parts and what they are is important, but knowing what they mean to you is even more important!

Rank all of your parts in order of importance to yourself. The most important part should be at the top of your list. This process will take time and negotiation. You must be totally open and honest in regard to which parts really belong at the top of your list. You will be surprised by your results!

This is an important step because it forms the foundation for "Your Pathway" to your blissful life. It is the basis on which the remainder of your journey stands!

Focus and take your time on this. There is no need to hurry. You will repeat this part of the process many times before creating your final list. This step may take hours, days, weeks or even months. Why? Because we all place varying degrees of importance on our parts. It is also during this leg of your journey that you will identify what you are willing to compromise for each part. Remember, you are only negotiating with *yourself*, so there are only winners here!

This was a very enlightening and exciting leg of my journey. I had finally given myself permission to rank my parts according to their importance to me, as opposed to their importance to others. I had finally "unlearned" old habits and was now about to draw the map for the rest of my life. Wow! Another "Ah-Ha!" moment for me. It was very freeing.

Once I had completed my rankings, I was pleasantly surprised at some of the results. I was not surprised that certain parts ranked so highly but, rather, I finally recognized what I really wanted versus how I had been living. I am confident that this exercise will be just as freeing for you.

List your parts in order of importance.

6

Your Acceptance

You have now defined your blissful life as it pertains to you. No one will have exactly the same definition as you. You have reached a milestone that most people never attain. The milestone is clearly defining exactly what you want in every part of your life. Most focus only on one or two parts of their lives. They typically only define what they want for those parts that are directly in front of them at that moment. Some never even define what they want! They simply let life drag them along. I compare this to going on vacation without an itinerary or a destination. You, on the other hand, have just defined what you want for every part of your life.

Notice how good you feel at this moment. Look back at your work and think about all of the parts you hadn't given much thought to in the past or were struggling with for some time. Read what you have written about these parts. Does what you have written give you clarity for that part? How do you feel about having this clarity? Those that I have worked with in the past have felt relief, a sense of calm, happiness, satisfaction, and even joy because they now had a clearer understanding of who they really are and where they really want to go. Revel in your feelings, for this is how you will live the rest of your life! Feel how good it feels to be free from the stress, anxiety, confusion and frustration of not having clarity. Reward yourself! Treat yourself to a special something for all of your hard work.

You need to do two more things before you begin moving toward your blissful life.

First, review all that you have completed so far:

1. Identifying all of your parts
2. Defining what you want your life to be like in each part you identified
3. Ranking your parts in order of importance to you

As you review your accomplishments from each step above, feel free to make any necessary adjustments. These adjustments can be identifying new parts, making deeper discoveries about a part, redefining a part, and even re-ranking your parts. This is *your* personal journey. You are the only person who determines whether it fits you. Making adjustments is another sign of the growth and discovery you are experiencing.

Now, take another look at your blissful life. Pretend you are in a beautiful, colorful hot air balloon. I am sure that you have seen the awesome pictures from the hot air balloon festival they have in New Mexico every year. They are all different shapes and sizes and come in an infinite number of colors. Notice how some are red, green, yellow and orange. Note the many different shapes of the balloons: round, oval and teardrop shapes. Notice the different sizes of the baskets: square, rectangular or round. See the different material the baskets are made from: metal, wicker and woven.

Close your eyes now and imagine that you are in one of the balloons. Feel the cool breeze on your skin and hear the hot air being blown into the balloon to keep you aloft. Look down as you begin to rise above the trees, fields and streams. See how the houses get smaller and smaller as you see angles of the land you could never see before! Notice how peaceful the landscape looks from above. Notice how the cars are moving, but no one seems to be in a rush. See the children playing in the yards. Notice how you can see the wildlife but cannot hear them. Finally, see yourself in your blissful life below you. Once you are in your balloon above the ground, continue with this chapter.

Now, as you float above your blissful life seeing yourself in it, take note of everything about you, things you see, sounds you hear, the feelings you are experiencing that you didn't before you defined your blissful life. Answer the following questions for each individual part.

What is different about you?

Are you smiling?

Are you laughing?

How do you feel?

Are you enjoying your blissful life?

Repeat this process for each part of your blissful life. When you are satisfied with this list, your blissful life is clearly defined.

The final step before moving forward is your acceptance of your blissful life. Accept the fact that yes, you can indeed be blissful! Give yourself permission to be blissful. It is sitting right there in front of you. Give yourself permission to reach out and embrace it. Many of my clients describe the first time they permit themselves to be blissful as being like a warm blanket on a cold winter night sitting next to a fireplace while others describe it as jumping into a pool on a hot summer's day. In both cases they were amazed at how enjoyable it was once they gave themselves permission to be blissful. You must be in total agreement with yourself, for every part of yourself, in every feeling about yourself. Allow yourself to experience your newly defined blissfulness.

Once you fully accept your blissful life, you can begin to define a course of action, commit to your course, and achieve your blissful life.

For me, acceptance took some time. It took many months to give myself permission to truly embrace the life I so desired. I was changing in so many ways and so quickly. I was enjoying it but, at the same time, I was struggling to give myself the permission to seek out my blissful life. There wasn't a single "Ah-Ha" moment for me here. No, it was the realization that in order to achieve the happiness that I truly desired in my life, I first had to be happy with *me*. I had accepted that what I wanted for me was okay. Nobody had ever said that to me before...or at least I wasn't hearing it. It was only after my total acceptance of my blissful life that I was able to continue on my path and take action toward achieving my blissful life.

Have you totally accepted your blissful life?
If not, repeat the work in this chapter until you do.

**How do you feel differently about
yourself now that you accept your blissful life?**

What does feeling this way enable you to do now, that you couldn't do before?

7

Your Commitment

Now that you have specifically defined your blissful life, you must take the first step in the walk toward the life you want. Just as when you take a walk through the park, on the beach or around the neighborhood, you must take the initiative in order to get where it is you want to go.

This step toward the life you desire greatly requires making a personal commitment to achieving it. Doing this is much more than simply stating you are committed to achieving it. You must execute a personal contract with yourself. A personal contract is your way of promising and documenting for yourself exactly what you are going to do and when you will do it. Stating your goal is only dreaming; writing your goals down and committing to them using your personal contract is called goal-setting.

Signing your personal contract clearly states that you are committed to achieving your blissful life. You will likely overcome all obstacles and roadblocks, regardless of origin, in achieving your blissful life. Many studies over the years have shown that those who write down and personally commit to their goals achieve them more than 80% of the time, versus those who merely state them.

So, whom should you share your personal contract with to ensure you achieve your goal? This is a serious question. No matter whom you share it with, you must be willing to permit them to hold you accountable if you are to achieve your blissful life. This person will be your accountability partner for the journey. They, too, must be willing to tell you what you *need* to hear, not necessarily what you *want* to hear. Their job in this process is to assist you, using any means necessary, in reaching your goal. Sometimes that means encouragement, at other times a good kick in the seat of the pants. This is the reason most people prefer a complete stranger as their accountability partner rather than a family member or friend. In either case, you must give them permission to hold you accountable for reaching your goals.

The accountability partner I chose was a coach I had come to know through my discovery phase. I wanted someone who would be willing to kick me if necessary, and yet still be supportive of my efforts. This individual was the perfect person for me. We worked out an arrangement that would compensate them for their time and was affordable for myself. It was at this moment that I had finally committed myself to achieving my blissful life. Up until this moment, I had merely done lip service to achieving it. The journey to your blissful life can be fun and exciting, while at other times it will be difficult. My accountability partner really helped me through those difficult times.

If you select an accountability partner and the relationship isn't working for you, don't worry. Just let your accountability partner know that the fit isn't what you need it to be. The two of you can adjust how you are working together, or perhaps you can even find a new accountability partner. This is a very common occurrence. The fact that the relationship needs to be adjusted or another accountability partner chosen does not reflect on either one of you. It merely demonstrates that you need a partner that is more useful for you. This is the same reason that some people drive red cars, others drive blue ones and still others drive yellow ones. Neither is better than the other, they are just different. It's okay!

I initially attempted to execute my personal contract by myself. What I found was that I was constantly finding myself off-track. Why? There are many reasons. It is very easy to do this because of your comfort with your existing patterns or habits. You see, as you begin executing your personal contract, you are re-training yourself. My tendency was to go back to what I knew…to what was easy and safe. Unfortunately, it was not what I wanted! It was at this point that I realized I needed assistance in achieving my blissful life. I immediately began my search for assistance.

The first step in this search was to make a list for the type of person I needed. Just like buying a car, you have to know what you want before you can go shopping. If you don't, they all look alike and you end up more confused than before you left the house. The same is true of coaches. If you don't make a list for the type of accountability partner you need, you will get confused very quickly.

Here is how I determined what type of accountability partner I needed. The first step was to identify the times when I tended to move toward my old unwanted patterns. I then noted what behaviors I was seemingly repeating. I also noted what goal the behaviors were preventing me from achieving. Next to each behavior, I noted how it was preventing me from reaching my goal. I then noted what I needed from an accountability partner that would prevent me from repeating my unwanted behavior. The third step was to take all of the required action items of the accountability partner and listed them on a single sheet of paper. This became my list of requirements for finding an accountability partner. I now had a list by which I could measure each potential partner.

I could now begin my search. I reviewed a list of family and friends. However, when I reviewed what I wanted and, more importantly, what I needed, I felt it best to look outside this circle. I then reviewed my network contacts. My network included many local coaches who are all very talented, each in their own unique way. I then listed out each coach's unique talents and abilities as I saw them. Some of them matched up nicely with my list. However, my intuition was telling me that I needed to look outside of this group as well. I have learned to trust my intuition because it is never wrong...neither is yours. It comes from deep within oneself and is always striving to protect and guide you.

As a result, I eliminated the local coaches with whom I already had a relationship. I then developed a list of individuals outside of my local area with which I had some prior contact. It did not matter that I had interacted with them on a completely different level. It only mattered that I believed they would be useful for me as an accountability partner. I then repeated the process of listing their unique abilities and measured this against my desired list of qualities. Luckily for me, I identified a potential partner from this list. I immediately contacted them. We discussed the purpose for my call and the journey that I was currently on. I asked them if they would be interested in being my accountability partner for the journey. They were flattered that I asked and stated that they would be delighted to assist me. We then discussed and arranged for an appropriate level of compensation for their time and effort. We then set guidelines for how we would work together so that I would get what I needed.

Finally, we set up a set schedule for when we would interact on a consistent basis. The key here is consistency. Both of you must commit to making it happen. If either party fails to commit, you are wasting each other's time. If you are the person that fails to commit, your partner should let you know this as soon as possible so that the two of you can determine the cause of the problem. Depending upon the reason, you may need to find another partner. Again, this is okay! It is no one's fault; you simply need a more useful partnership.

If you cannot find an accountability partner at this point, you will want to consider using one of the many resources available on the Internet today. There are many established organizations that oversee the certifications and standards for the coaching industry. Some of these organizations include The International Coaching Federation, International Association of Coaches, Coachville.com, 247coaching.com and CMT International. You can also do a simple Internet search. The key here is to continue searching until you find an accountability partner who is right for you.

Let's review:

1. State your specific goals for each part in a positive manner.
2. Document your goals in your personal contract.
3. Commit to your goals by signing your personal contract.
4. Share your personal contract with an accountability partner.

For your convenience, you can find a copy of a personal contract at the back of this book. Additionally, you may also download an electronic version from www.timothymcginty.com/BlissfulLife/PersonalContract.htm

What does completing your Personal Contract mean to you?

Who are the most likely candidates to be your accountability partner and why?

When will you talk to your potential accountability partners? Set a deadline for yourself for speaking with them and for taking the action of selecting an accountability partner. This will help keep you moving forward.

8

Your Action

Now that you have committed to achieving your goals and have determined if you require an accountability partner to reach them, it is time to develop your course of action. Exactly how do you plan to get from your current location to your blissful life? What course must you chart to achieve it? At first glance, this question may seem overwhelming. However, when we break it down as we will in the following pages, you will see exactly how easy this will be. This course will lead you to your promised land. Also, you will enjoy taking action because you know exactly where you're headed to your blissful life!

Developing your course of action is an easy process. It is much like planning a vacation. Everyone enjoys planning for vacation! If you are like most individuals, you probably plan a vacation every year. This process involves choosing a destination (which you have already done), planning how you will get there (plane, car, train, etc.), how long you will stay and when you will return. The best part about your current journey is the fact that it is a one-way trip! You are headed to complete satisfaction, in every "part" of your life. You can forget about a return trip. Once you are there, you won't ever want to return to where you are now! Where you are headed is so much better!

To develop your course of action, repeat the following for each of your parts:

1. Select the part you will focus upon according to your parts ranking in **Chapter 5: Your Discovery.**

2. Review the desired outcome for the part you have selected. Now the fun begins.

3. In a moment, you will go forward in your own personal time machine: your mind! That's right, one of your many hidden talents will allow you to travel through time in your mind to see, hear and feel yourself having already achieved your goal! Doing this is very easy. You already have all the tools you need to experience it. If you like, have your accountability partner walk you through this exercise. Now get yourself into a comfortable position, such as sitting in your favorite chair or relaxing on your couch. The key is to be comfortable. Now, close your eyes and relax. Take a deep breath through your nose, hold it for a few seconds and slowly exhale through your mouth. As you exhale, feel how relaxed your mind and body are. With every breath you take, your body expels all thoughts, worries and tension you might be experiencing. Take another deep breath through your nose, hold it for a few seconds, and slowly exhale again through your mouth. Notice how loose and free your legs and arms have become. Also notice how relaxed your neck and shoulders are. Take your third deep breath, hold it in, and then exhale slowly through your mouth. Notice how relaxed your torso has become. Your heart rate has slowed considerably. You are now in a totally relaxed state. Enjoy how good it feels to be so relaxed. Your mind and body are quiet. Now, picture yourself in the future having already achieved your goal for this part. Notice how you look, what you are saying, and that special feeling you have right now.

4. Take a look back at the present, taking note of all that you have done to get where you are currently standing, having achieved your goal. What specific actions did you take? What specific thoughts did you think? How did your feelings about yourself change? What are others saying about you? Jot down your answers on a sheet of paper. Take note of every action, thought and feeling.

    Now, slowly come back into the moment, into the present. Leave your totally relaxed state behind. You are now completely refreshed. Remain seated or lying down for a few moments until you are fully back in the present moment.

5. Take another sheet of paper and restate the items you noted in Step 4 above in the following manner: for each action you imagined yourself taking, restate it as an action to be taken. Review the notes about how you will think about yourself. Do you need to take any actions to begin thinking about yourself in that manner? If you noted a change in your thoughts about yourself, create an action item stating that you must start thinking about yourself in the manner you noted. What did others say to you? Do you need to create any action items from the comments they made to you or about you?

6. Determine which actions you took first in order to achieve your goal. You can rank them by numbering them in the margin. Continue down the list until all items have been given a number. This is your Action Item List.

7. Repeat this process for a maximum of three parts.

    NOTE: *Attempting to focus on more than three parts leads to an unfocused journey. Individuals who attempt this path find they become lost and confused. Keep your action plain...keep it focused.*

8. Once you have your prioritized your Item List, review it with your accountability partner. He or she should talk with you to ensure that you are certain of the prioritization of your tasks. This is where your accountability partner's work begins. They need to hold you accountable for completing your Action Item List so that you can achieve your goals. You must verbalize to your partner that you give them permission to hold you accountable for getting what you want. They must also commit and verbalize to you that they will hold you accountable.

9. Set up a meeting schedule with your accountability partner. This meeting will be at whatever frequency (weekly, bi-weekly or monthly, etc.) that you need in order to keep you on your path. The key here is consistency. You both must commit to the schedule and hold each other to it. During these meetings you will review your progress, discuss areas in which you may be struggling or need to learn new strategies and what items from your Action Item List need to be moved into focus. I am confident that if you have successfully selected an accountability partner that is right for you, they will assist you in discovering what you need to do to eliminate any struggles, as well as discovering the new strategies you require to achieve your goals.

The above process assists you in developing an achievable action plan. As you move toward and achieve your goals, select your next part and add its action items to your action list. This ensures that you are always moving, listening and feeling the power of moving toward your goals. Using this process is so easy because you want nothing more than to achieve your goals.

The single most amazing thing about this entire process is how easy it is to execute. The more you execute it, the easier it gets. Hour by hour, day by day, week by week and month by month, your journey becomes easier and easier and ever more satisfying. I enjoyed this part of the process immensely. Perhaps it was because my accountability partner had a prior background in Time Line work and was very good at it, or perhaps it was because I knew I was laying out my course for moving toward and getting exactly what I wanted, just the way I wanted it. Whatever the reason, I had fun with it.

Another thing about the process for me was how easy it was to imagine myself in the future having already achieved my goals and how clearly defined the path was I had taken to achieve it when I looked back to where I had been. I believe that the reason it was so easy for me to move into the future to see, hear and feel me already having achieved my goals is because I wanted them so deeply, so badly, so much more than anything else in the world. My subconscious mind was just waiting for me to give it permission to go there. I had to move my conscious mind aside and allow my subconscious mind to explore. Once there, I looked back to where I had been and could see exactly what I had done to get to where I wanted to be. My accountability partner noted all of these items as I noted and described them to him. This became the basis for my action plan. It was so easy. I couldn't believe it! I had struggled with all of this for so many years and, finally, right there in front of me, there it was! An "Ah-Ha!" moment for me for sure!

Once I came down off my "Ah-Ha" cloud, my accountability partner and I developed my Action Item List. I couldn't wait to get moving. I had waited for so long. My issue, just like so many others, is that I wanted everything to get done *yesterday*. What I soon realized is that everything had to be done in order. The reason is that you, just as I did, will learn something on each step of the journey. The lessons learned while completing my current action items put me into proper alignment for moving forward. This ensures that at each step you have exactly what you need in order to succeed! I could not rush the process. I quickly learned to slow down and enjoy the journey because it held many experiences and lessons that I needed to learn in order to get what I want. So, don't rush it. Live each moment, taking away all that you can while learning all that you need. You will succeed.

How do you feel about your action plan? Are you comfortable with it? If not, repeat the process in this chapter until you are completely satisfied with it.

Write how you felt as you executed the process. What was easy for you? Were there any parts of the process that challenged you? If so, how did they challenge you?

What did you learn about yourself going through the process?

What three parts are you focusing on and why?

Your Achievement

Your achievement is present in every step you make while en route to your goals. Every step, every move, every feeling you experience should be recognized and celebrated. These come in many different forms. You must learn to recognize your achievements. When you first began reading this book, you may have been frustrated, depressed, angry, etc. The simple fact that you picked up this book and committed to improving yourself shows you achieved something, you took action. Did you know you are made of up as many parts as you noted? Did you know what you wanted for your parts? Were you committed before you started reading this book? If you have moved forward in any manner whatsoever, you have achieved! How do you feel when you look at all of the work you have accomplished? You are moving, growing and expanding yourself, and this is significant for you!

Celebrating your achievements is extremely important to your continued success and progress. So, how should you celebrate your success? I recommend selecting a thing or place that puts you on top of the world. Something you enjoy more than anything else. Reward yourself! You've earned it! The more you reward yourself for your successes, the more this feeling will be associated with moving toward achieving your goals. This awesome feeling becomes so desirous that you will move toward it again and again, closer and closer, achieving more and more goals. You will amaze yourself how quickly and easily you move toward your blissful life.

Think of your recognition of your achievements as carrots are to a racehorse. The race horse enjoys the carrots so much that they will continually run towards them until they reach the carrot, their reward for running. They enjoy them so much they will always move towards them. The reward is more than worth the journey! The same holds true for you. The more you recognize and celebrate your achievements, the easier and more enjoyable it is to continue moving towards your blissful life. What could be more rewarding than achieving your blissful life?

Imagine how you will feel when you reach your personal pot of gold, your Emerald City as in *The Wizard of Oz*! Others will watch in total amazement as they see you transition toward who you want to be and where you want to go. The best part is that even if no one else notices, you will know that you have arrived at the life you want to live and the person that you want to be because you can measure it against your goals! You'll be able to go down your checklist of goals and check them off as achieved, all the while smiling and enjoying it.

I rewarded myself in numerous ways throughout my journey. For smaller accomplishments, I rewarded myself with a nice gift. This would typically be something that I wanted, but might not normally purchase. These items ranged from dinner at a nice restaurant to buying CDs or MP3s. Sometimes I simply gave myself permission to take an afternoon off to go enjoy the park or the lake, the bonus to this reward being that I typically do my most focused thinking and deepest reflection when I connect with nature. For larger accomplishments, I rewarded myself with larger items. Not necessarily more expensive items, but in terms if importance to me.

Sometimes I would go camping for a weekend near Ohio's Lake Erie Islands. Other times, I would take time off and simply lie round by the pool for the weekend. The most enjoyable of all the rewards I gave myself was to simply sit back and enjoy my newfound blissfulness. I noticed how my attitude towards myself, others, and the environment around me had changed. I would sit back and note how much more I appreciated everyone and everything around me. It was as though I was seeing them through a new set of eyes! This was the best reward for me because it was the one which lasted longest and was deepest felt.

It didn't matter what the reward was, as long as it was enjoyable and important. I recognized I deserved the reward: I had worked hard, allowed myself to be open to growth and experience and moved along my path toward my ultimate goal of a blissful life. Reward yourself, you've earned it!

What are things you enjoy doing but never seem to have the time to do?

What are some things you'd like to have, but won't buy for yourself?

When was the last time you stopped to smell the roses?

How much do you appreciate those around you?

How has your world changed since you started reading this book?

How have your feelings about yourself changed since you started reading this book?

10

Your Changes

You will experience change as you continually achieve and then redefine your blissful life and what it means to you. Just like yourself, your blissful life is a dynamic, ever-changing definition. These changes typically come in waves like the low and high tides of the ocean. Some people experience them on a regular basis while others experience them less often. One thing is certain though, you *will* experience them, so embrace your changes as they represent your growth toward new goals, expanding your mind, body and spirit...your entire world.

In this instance, change is good. Many times, individuals will view change as a bad thing because they are uncertain of how to deal with it. As a result of their uncertainty, they resist change. They are so uncertain they fight change at every moment. As a result, any change will quickly send their life and world spinning out of control. If they were to take the time and recognize change for what it is...growth, learning and experience...they would soon realize that it isn't all that bad. They would recognize the lesson to be learned and how the universe was challenging them to challenge themselves to grow in some manner.

Once recognized, one can then easily integrate this into their lives. People successfully do this every day and integrate these changes into their lives without even thinking about it. Why? They trust and allow their subconscious mind to absorb all that it needs in order for them to move forward and grow. They know their subconscious mind is always protecting and doing what is best for them at that moment. Their subconscious mind views these changes and only allows those useful for being integrated into their lives. They experience, learn and grow without even thinking about it. They automatically have a system defined for them which dictates when and how to learn and integrate. These people tend to take any required action automatically. Many of their friends will call them special, gifted or even lucky.

You, by virtue of reading this book, know exactly what action you need to take in order to integrate your new or redefined goals. Your process for integrating change is now defined and can even be referenced as required. Simply reach for this book, review Chapter 8: "Your Action," and walk through the process you have used in the past. Luckily, regardless of what type of individual you are, you have a process defined for yourself. It doesn't matter which process you use, either works fine. It is this experience that provides you comfort in knowing that you will achieve your new goals because both processes work. Your outcome will be exactly what you want. As long as you follow the process, you can achieve exactly what you desire. That's right, everything you want, just the way you want it. Many people believe this is false. The reason they don't believe it is because they have not focused on themselves and clearly defined what they want and their plan for achieving it. Hence, they form a belief that they will never have what they want because they don't know exactly what that is!

Since my initial discovery of my blissful life, I have experienced a tremendous amount of growth. This growth has impacted just about every part of my being over the last three years. However, I am totally comfortable with the impact of this because I...just as you do now...had the tools to apply the changes to each respective part to ensure that my goal for that part was very clear. I then ensured that these new goals were congruent with my other parts. Finally, I reviewed my personal action plan to determine if I needed to make any adjustments based on my new goals for myself. Where I used to shy away from change, I now embrace it. Change is an indication that I am forever growing and learning and expanding as the unique individual that I am. I do not place limits on myself and this has allowed me to expand and grow at an accelerated rate. This is exactly what I defined for my student part. I am, and forever will be, a student of life. Regardless of the growth or the area in which I grow, I use the above process to integrate change in my life. Which process I utilize depends upon a number of items such as how I am feeling at that moment, what part of my journey I am on, what part is being impacted and the change itself. You too will continually grow and change as you move towards your blissful life. I encourage you to be totally open to your personal growth and, ultimately, change. Once you define the change and what it means to you, integrate it to ensure you remain congruent.

I recommend that you, at a minimum, review your growth annually. Some individuals review their goals quarterly. Some like to revisit their goals on a monthly basis. Others, like myself, revisit their goals and integrate any changes on an as-needed basis. When I feel a shift occur within, it is a change indicator for me. It indicates that I need to rest, recognize the changes, integrate them, and make any necessary adjustments in my plan. This enables me to ensure that my goals are always accurate. You will get to the point in your life, just as I have, where the recognition, integration and adjustments occur almost naturally, without much effort. It becomes this simple because you utilize the process so often that it becomes second nature. As I said before, you are forever changing and growing. How you deal with your growth determines if you are able to remain happy throughout your life.

How do you view change now versus how you viewed change before reading this chapter?

What limits, if any, that you place on yourself prevent you from changing?

What do you need to do to eliminate these limits?

How do you feel knowing that you can and will achieve your blissful life?

How will you revisit your growth and goals?

11

Your Integration

Anyone who has spent any time focused on self-improvement or self-growth has heard the word "integration." But what does it mean? Is it another process? It is an action? What does it mean to *you*? Actually, integration is all of those things rolled into one. *Webster's Dictionary* defines integration as, "The act of combining into an integral whole." Ultimately, because we are all unique individuals, every individual defines integration as it relates to them. Some define integration as a process or specific action. However you define your integration, it is the essence of how you meld and weave your new features into your existing core. So, how do you integrate your changes? What works for one person may be less useful for another. Just as we are all unique individuals, our integrations are also unique. One thing is certain: integration is a good thing, as it leads to a new and improved you!

The objective of integration is to find that balance between your mind, body and spirit in a manner that is most useful for you. It is that easy, peaceful feeling you have when you are in complete balance. Many people utilize meditation, others prayer, and still others a conscious effort to realize this balance. This book actually incorporates a process within the process of defining your blissful life, enabling you to naturally integrate your changes. As long as you take action to achieve your blissful life, your integration will take place. This is because you consciously defined your goals for every part of yourself. Next, you checked to ensure that your goals for each part were congruent with your other parts. This process is a step of integration, ensuring that your mind, body, and spirit are congruent. Finally, you defined your action plan to achieve your blissful life. This enabled you to define the actions you needed to take in order to achieve your blissful life all the while ensuring that your mind, body and spirit were in congruence. As such, you define your own integration.

After much struggling, I attended a retreat that introduced me to a process for stepping into the future and looking back toward the now in order to discover what I needed to do to achieve that which I wanted. I could clearly see exactly what I needed to do to get here. While this formed the foundation of the integration process used in this book, I enhanced the process for even greater impact. I focus on a single part at a time and note all of the items I discovered. I would be very clear and specific about what I needed to do to achieve all that I wanted for that part of myself. After I was done with all my parts, I had many pieces of paper, each with its own action plan. I then reviewed all of them and noted any common actions so that I would know how many separate parts would be impacted by specific actions. I also prioritized which parts were most important to me and then focused on my top three. Since my action plans were already defined, all I had to do was act!

When I discovered my blissful life, I actually spent a great deal of time not only discovering and defining exactly what it was that I wanted for each part of myself, but also how I was going to integrate these things into my life. I did not use the framework defined in this book to help me. As a result, I was actually quite lost for a time, searching for a method of integration that was most useful. I had defined my blissful life, but what was I going to do with it? How was I going to use this to change my life? What did I need to do to achieve it? How was I going to get from where I was at to where I truly wanted to be? I struggled for a long time. My blissful life was a radical shift from where I was before my discovery. It was, without a doubt, a life-changing event.

It was at this point that I developed the process for this book. The process I defined incorporates integration at every step in the process. This enables you to avoid the struggle I had to deal with in my own integration. You have already begun integrating changes into your life! All you need to do is execute your action plan and your integration will be complete.

What actions have you already taken towards executing your action plan?

What parts of your life has your integration already begun?

How does it feel to be integrating your changes into your life?

12 Your New Place

Welcome home! Welcome to your blissful life. So, tell me, what does it look like? Why do you sound so different? How does it feel to achieve that what you have been searching for so long? This is your new and improved life. Words can hardly express how you feel at this moment. Like the movie star who just received their first Oscar, you cry. Look back at where you came from and all that you have achieved to be in your new place. Wow!

You are much like the old-time sailors. You left a safe and comfortable port (your old place) with the definition of a broad destination of where you were headed. You utilized this book, as well as other information, and defined your specific destination. You then charted your course of action. It provided you with the process and certainty you needed to continue sailing. This is much like the old maritime sailing charts. While sailing traditions provided a process, the destination was always determined by how the sailors utilized them. Once they began their journey, there was no turning back to port. Their desire to reach new and safer harbor was too great. Just as they sought new and exciting places, so did you. Your destination...your new place or your blissful life...was defined, and how you charted your course was the process you just completed and will maintain on a continual basis. The closer you got, the more focused, specific and determined you became towards reaching it.

Enjoy your new place, your blissful life. It is your personal Garden of Eden. Look around you and notice how all of the colors are brighter, more vibrant! Listen to the birds and hear the songs they are singing in your honor! What is that song? How happy are you at this very moment? This is how every day will be for the rest of your life. You will enjoy every moment of every day because you now feel, hear and see things in a new and more useful way. You look forward to every day and all that it offers you.

Even when faced with what others perceive as bad or stressful situations, you remain blissful because you now know how each moment or event fits into your life! Your knowledge enables you to deal with these events in a manner that is more useful for you. You realize that they are merely teaching something that you need to know or experience. You now take these lessons and experiences and enjoy them for what they are...lessons and experiences. Where others see limitations, you see opportunity. Where they feel pain or depression, you feel a sense of tranquility and hope. Where they hear others calling them back, you hear joyous music urging you forward.

Is it possible to be any happier than you are right now? I didn't think so! When I finally achieved my blissful life, it felt as though I had finally reached what I had been searching for my entire life. I was finally blissful! No longer was a part of me missing. I now knew exactly what I wanted my life to be, how I wanted to live it and who I wanted in it. I am still on cloud nine!

Awaken every day and be thankful for all that you will experience today. You probably cannot wait to get moving and experience all life has to offer. Who will you meet today? What will you learn today? Who will you help today? What gifts will the universe offer you? You are a powerful force within this universe and you can do and achieve all that you dream. Wow! Every evening, reflect back on your day so that you do not miss anything. Be thankful for all that you have experienced, learned and received. Finally, take a step back and realize how this day fits into your future. How is it preparing you for tomorrow? By doing so, you better understand all that you have experienced and how it fits into your grand plan.

I never knew just how great life could feel. I am truly in awe of all that I have become and all that I have. I am amazed at how everything I experience and learn prepares me for the next step in my journey of life. I love today and cannot wait for tomorrow!

Now go and enjoy your blissful life! You have all you need to live life like you never have before. Enjoy!

How do you feel about yourself and your life right now?

How are you different now that you have completed the process?

Epilogue

Congratulations, and thank you for taking the time to read and experience my book. Thank you for allowing me to be a part of your experience and to assist you in discovering your blissful life. That which you previously thought was so far away was actually hiding within you, just waiting to be released. Your inner self knew exactly what it was you wanted and was just waiting for you to give it permission to share it. You already had all that you needed to get what you wanted, you just had to realize it and open up to allow yourself to discover it. Enjoy it, every second of every minute of every hour of every day of every month of every year. I know exactly how you are feeling because I am feeling it, too.

If this book has impacted your life, why keep it to yourself? Share all that you have learned with someone who may be struggling. You now know how powerful the process was for you and you can give them the greatest gift of all...your love and guidance. You, too, will experience the joy and incredibly powerful feeling of positively impacting another's life by simply buying them this book or recommending they attend one of my workshops or listen to one of my DVDs. You can find them both on my Web site at www.timothymcginty.com.

Blessings and hugs,

Timothy A. McGinty

About The Author

Timothy A. McGinty is a public speaker and author who provides success coaching for businesses, executives and individuals. He is a Master Practitioner of Neuro-Linguistic Programming (NLP), Accredited Master Mentor through CMT International Ltd., and an Accredited Associate of the Insitute for Independent Business in Watford, England.

He is also a Certified Innermetrix Consultant, Certified DiSC Facilitator, Certified Emotional Endurance Coach, Certified NLP Life Coach, Licensed NLP Neuro-Natural Health Specialist, Licensed NLP Timeline Coach, Regression Specialist, licensed Hypnotherapist and a Reiki Master. He is also a co-author in *Wake Up...Live the Life You Love*, Wake Up Moments with Dr. Wayne Dyer, Brian Tracy, Steven E and many other leaders in the coaching profession. Mr. McGinty also holds a Bachelor of Science Degree in Computer and Information Science with a concentration in Accounting from Cleveland State University.

Today, Mr. McGinty lives in northeast Ohio, where he was born and raised. He lives there with his wife Susan and their three dogs: Zoe, Gunner and Jazz. After starting a number of businesses and achieving personal success, he set out to assist others in achieving their own. He exited his prior businesses and has subsequently focused solely on coaching activities for the past several years. He assists clients in "closing the gap" between their potential and their actual performance in helping them achieve their dreams! He utilizes only proven strategies and methodologies to ensure his clients get there faster. His products and services include one-on-one coaching, workshops, seminars, public speaking, CDs, DVDs and his own writings.

Resources

Imagine Yourself
13477 Prospect Rd. Suite 204
Strongsville, OH 44149
Ph: (440) 785-7950
tim@timothymcginty.com
www.timothymcginty.com

Bennett-Stellar University
6930 132nd St. SE
Snohomish, WA 98296
Ph: 206-729-8658
bestu@imagineit.org
www.imagineit.org

Bibliography

Bennett Stellar University. *Subconscious Communcation, Neuro-Linguistic Hypnotherapy Course Module #102*. Washington: Bennett Stellar University.

Your *Blissful* Life
PERSONAL CONTRACT

Name: _____   Date: _____

This Personal Contract acknowledges my commitment to achieving my blissful life for each part I have defined below. By signing this contract, I commit to myself that I will take action everyday towards getting the life I desire.

I hereby also authorize my accountability partner to hold me accountable for achieving the goals I have defined in this contract. I recognize that my accountability partner will be forthright and honest with me at all times. I also commit to being forthright and honest with my accountability partner and give my partner permission to hold me accountable for achieving my goals, no matter what!

As your accountability partner, I commit to holding you accountable for achieving you're the goals you have defined in your Personal Contract. Additionally, I commit to not judging you and being completely honest with you at all times, no matter what!

The following pages clearly define the various parts and the goals for these parts that I am focusing on at this time. We will update the parts and goals to be focused on as I progress in achieving my goals for my various parts.

Part: _____
Goals for this part:

Part: _____
Goals for this part:

Your *Blissful* Life
PERSONAL CONTRACT CONTINUED

Part: _____
Goals for this part:

Signed: _____

Accountability Partner: _____

Date: _____

www.ingramcontent.com/pod-product-compliance
Lightning Source LLC
Chambersburg PA
CBHW020008050426
42450CB00005B/368